VINTAGE
Quilt Treasures
1930s REVISITED

Anne Dutton

A Q S American Quilter's Society
www.AmericanQuilter.com

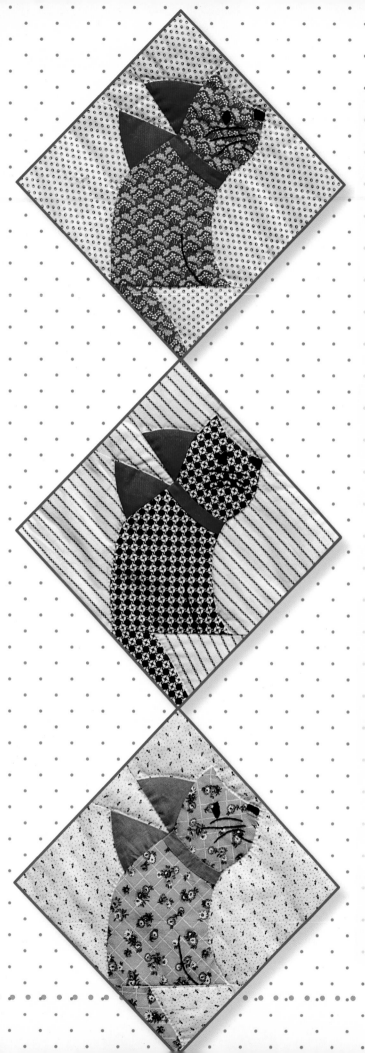

The American Quilter's Society or AQS is dedicated to quilting excellence. AQS promotes the triumphs of today's quilter, while remaining dedicated to the quilting tradition. AQS believes in the promotion of this art and craft through AQS Publishing and AQS QuiltWeek®.

DIRECTOR OF PUBLICATIONS: KIMBERLY HOLLAND TETREV
ASSISTANT EDITOR: ADRIANA FITCH
CONTENT/TECHNICAL EDITOR: CAITLIN TETREV
PROOFING EDITOR: SARAH BOZONE
ILLUSTRATIONS: ELAINE WILSON
GRAPHIC DESIGN: ELAINE WILSON
COVER DESIGN: MICHAEL BUCKINGHAM
QUILT PHOTOGRAPHY: CHARLES R. LYNCH

Additional copies of this book may be ordered from the American Quilter's Society, PO Box 3290, Paducah, KY 42002-3290, or online at www.ShopAQS.com.

Attention Photocopying Service: Please note the following—Publisher and author give permission to print pages 16–19, 22–25, 28–31, and 47.

American Quilter's Society

www.AmericanQuilter.com

Library of Congress Cataloging-in-Publication Data

Names: Dutton, Anne, 1941- author.
Title: Vintage quilt treasures : 1930s revisited / By Anne Dutton.
Description: Paducah, KY : American Quilter's Society, 2016.
Identifiers: LCCN 2015042241 (print) | LCCN 2015042785 (ebook) | ISBN 9781604604023 (pbk.) | ISBN 9781604603279 ()
Subjects: LCSH: Patchwork--Patterns. | Quilting--Patterns.
Classification: LCC TT835 .D89 2016 (print) | LCC TT835 (ebook) | DDC 746.46--dc23
LC record available at http://lccn.loc.gov/2015042241

COVER QUILT AND LEFT: SCRAPPY CAT, detail. Full quilt on page 60.

TITLE PAGE: SCRAPPY GIRLS, detail. Full quilt on page 54.

AKNOWLEDGEMENTS

I wish to thank my great-grandmother Frances Jane Waddell for her influence in my life. Although she passed before I was born, the gifts of her life have flowed down through the family.

The quilt designs in this book represent ones reminiscent of the early twentieth century. Fabrics that would have been used early on are just as impressive as the modern batiks of today. The patterns are timely and hopefully will continue to be for years to come.

My quilting group, Prime Time Quilters, has been so important in the design process. The technique of curved piecing is a challenge. My very dear friends have tested, suggested, and encouraged me as I sought to make this a process an enjoyable one.

Pat Roche has machine quilted most of the quilts, while Dorothy Dodds hand quilted one of them. I do appreciate their help and expertise.

INTRODUCTION

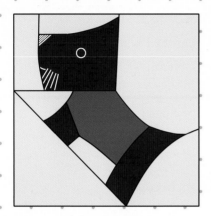

A Scottie Dog

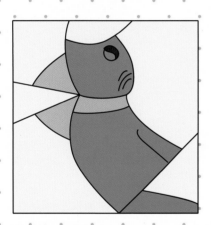

A Calico Cat

A Mighty Pretty Girl

What a pleasure it is to share these special patterns with you. They were found in my great-grandmother Frances Jane Waddell's trunk years after she passed. They were sent to me as a gift, packaged inside the original envelope in which they were mailed. My great-grandmother had ordered them through the Charlotte Observer newspaper in Charlotte, North Carolina.

Later, I received her eye glasses from an uncle. They showed signs of repair by my great-granddad. These treasures were important to him and now to me. I have enjoyed making and designing these quilts. My hope is you find them as special as I do.

Anne Dutton

CONTENTS

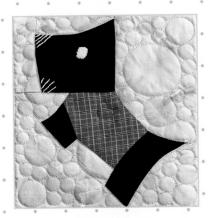

THE TREASURE

Frances Jane Waddell

Frances Jane Waddell was born June 16, 1872, and lived until January of 1940. She was a blessing to all who knew her. Under her inspiration and the hard work of her family, a new church, St. John's United Methodist was formed in 1935. It not only gave her a place to worship and teach, but was also a community of folks who helped her to carry out important needs during her time. They consisted of knitting sweaters for the soldiers in World War I and sewing groups that spent their time stitching new US flags and sewing Red Cross emblems.

She was my Great-Grandmother, known affectionately as Granny to all and was a poet who loved to write prose. She taught the boys in Sunday school and was an avid student of the Bible. She loved quilting and used patterns found in the newspaper to make some of my favorite designs, too. Her old cookbook highlights recipes that could feed crowds and had helpful hints written in the margins. In her latter years, when suffering with cancer, the family read the Scriptures to her. She was indeed a treasure, from her community to her family and for generations to come.

Her legacy has certainly touched many areas of my life and although she passed away before I was born, I feel a real kinship and love for Granny Waddell.

LEFT: Drawing of St. John's United Methodist Church, Charlotte, North Carolina drawn by the author's father, Ed Waddell, in 1947. He also built the church building.

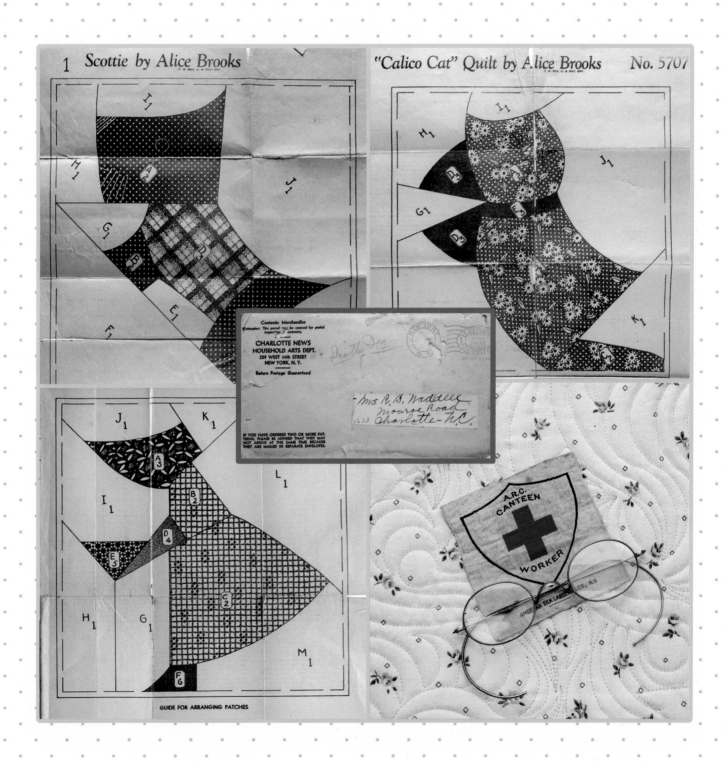

A Historical Note

What Anne Dutton received from her Great Grandmother was a treasured find. She in fact discovered the original patterns by Alice Brooks which had been issued via a mail order ad placed in the *Charlotte Observer*. She received patterns from Household Arts, Inc. which was incorporated September 26, 1933 and held the Alice Brooks needlework patterns byline. The patterns were received on a printed sheet about 17" x 27" and the instructions where either printed in the column or on another sheet. The purchaser received only these papers, in an envelope the ad was ordered from, and possibly the byline.

This is where the mystery of these patterns begin. Alice Brooks' patterns were all titled to give everyone the impression that she designed them. After much research, it turns out that the mystery of the actual designer may never be known, because Alice Brooks is a fictional person. The mystery continues with the origins of the companies that put the ads in the newspapers. Using numerous addresses and names for the patterns, it is very hard to track the exact origins. "The first of the group of New York City pattern companies responsible for the Laura Wheeler and Alice Brooks needlework patterns, the Anne Adams and Marian Martin clothing patterns, and others was incorporated August 13, 1928 and did not use a byline with its features in the beginning. As a group, the companies are a tangled web of names and addresses. From their inception, the features created by the various companies were distributed in the United States by King Features Syndicate, Inc., a division of the Hearst Corporation. King Features is represented in Canada by Star Newspaper Service / Toronto Star Syndicate," (Smith, Laura Wheeler and Alice Brooks).

Convention, at the time, was to use multiple names and addresses so the publisher, George Felleman Goldsmith, Jr. could put several patterns in the same newspaper and in competing newspapers.

The first appearance of patterns by Alice Brooks was in 1928. Then in 1933 the face of a woman was incorporated into the ads.

 No one knows the identity of this woman. It is possible this is the face of another woman that was listed among the many names and addresses in association with Household Arts. It is possible that she is Rae A. Goldsmith, wife of Reader Mail's founder, George F. Goldsmith, Jr. She is described in a 1930's census as a "pattern stylist." While there is no proof that Rae Goldsmith is the original creator, the theory is that Mrs. Goldsmith designed the patterns and that Mr. Goldsmith published them.

Citations

Alboum, Rose Lea. "The Quilts Designs Of Alice Brooks." *The American Legacy Quilt Index Series*. Rose Lea Alboum, 2006. Web. 23 Sept. 2015.

Smith, Wilene. "Laura Wheeler and Alice Brooks." *Quilt History Tidbits – Old & Newly Discovered*. Wilene Smith, 14 Sept. 2010. Web. 23 Sept. 2015.

Unknown. "Overview of Vintage Embroidery Transfers." *The Sewing Pallette*. Sewing Palette, Inc., 2005. Web. 23 Sept. 2015.

GENERAL DIRECTIONS

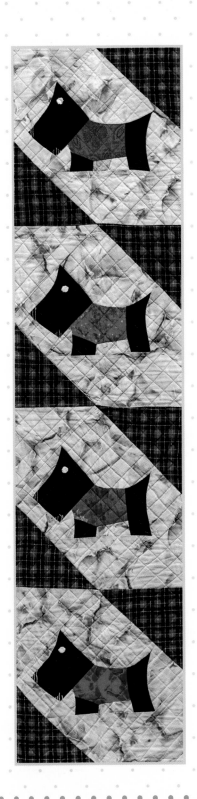

The following considerations are designed to instruct in precision piecing techniques. Whether by hand or machine, the techniques are the same. Curved seams require very special stitching. It is true that the focus blocks in this book will take time and patience to sew, but it is also true that the techniques learned and mastered will be an advantage for piecing needs for various quilting projects to be made in the future.

The Scottie Dog, Calico Cat, and A Mighty Pretty Girl are pieced and not appliquéd, this makes them very special. Each one includes some embroidery, but in some cases embellishments may be done with permanent fabric markers as well. Choose them wisely and test before using.

It is suggested that you make one of each block to learn precision. These test blocks can later be used for pillows or doll quilts.

My experience in teaching has shown me that when a student knows why the necessary steps are needed, it makes more sense and produces a better result. These are fussy little blocks, but extremely rewarding. So take the time, enjoy the process, and make something beautiful.

Coloring or Embroidery Suggestions

Each of the blocks requires embroidery. Pearl cotton size 8 or 3 strands of traditional embroidery floss is recommended. Permanent fabric markers can be used for the flowers. TEST first on a scrap fabric with washing and drying. Refer to the templates for areas to be colored.

RIGHT SCOTTIE IN PLAID, detail. Full quilt on page 57.

Selecting the Fabric

These patterns were designed in the 1930s and were made from feed sacks, gingham, or fabric called conversational prints. They are sold today as reproduction prints. I have shown one of the Calico Cat patterns made in those fabrics. Modern batiks are also a good choice. Fabric should be 100% cotton, prewashed, and pressed.

Making the Templates

Carefully cut out the templates along the solid lines. If making several blocks, transfer the templates to plastic to retain their shape. Notice the markings: solid lines for cutting, dashed lines for stitching, small dots for matching, arrow for straight of grain placement, and the identity of each piece by name, number, and fabric requirement. Words will appear on the right side of the template. If hand piecing, trim the seam allowance away from the template, and mark the stitching line on the wrong side of the fabric. Cut it out leaving ¼" of fabric from the stitching line all around the piece. Follow the marked stitching line when sewing.

Cutting Out the Pieces

Select fabric for each piece of the block and notice the straight-of-grain, which is parallel to the selvage. This is very important for ease in curved piecing. Draw around each piece with a very sharp #2 pencil on the wrong side of the fabric. It is risky cutting several layers, but if you choose to do so using a rotary cutter, make sure all layers are wrong side up. If using solid fabric mark the wrong side of the fabric as it is easy to reverse some pieces.

Stitching Considerations

Curved seams require great care to maintain the ¼" seam allowance. Imperfect seam allowance in each block compromises the overall size. Make a practice block first to test your skill. Each pieced block should measure 9½" x 9½".

When hand piecing, the stitching line is drawn on the wrong side of the fabric and the stitching can be seen on both sides as you sew along the lines. When machine piecing, the seam allowance must be followed along a marking on the machine. A quarter-inch foot or a tape marking on the machine under the presser foot is helpful. To mark the machine guide, place a ruler under the foot so that the quarter inch line is just under the needle. Place a piece of painter's tape (easy to remove) or move the needle position so that you can follow the edge of the presser foot.

A good test for a machine stitched quarter inch is as follows:

Cut (3) 2" x 8" strips of fabrics. Sew them together to form a strata that measures 5" x 8". Measure across the strata. The proper width should be 5". If not, make the adjustment to sew a narrower or wider seam to achieve the 5".

Curved Piecing Techniques

The success of curved piecing is in perfect cutting, perfect seam allowance of ¼", and in keeping the edges exactly together. In curved piecing, a concave curve is sewn to a convex curve. Place the concave curve on the bottom and layer the convex curve piece on the top. Mark the corner matching dots. Mark the center of each piece.

Do not sew into the seam allowance. This makes it easy to intersect other curved pieces and allows seams to be pressed in either direction, often toward the darker fabric.

It is easy to stretch the convex curve to fit the concave curve, but DO NOT. Match dot to dot, with the edges exactly aligned, and the piece should fit perfectly.

Pressing and Finishing the Block

Carefully press the completed block. Fold the seams toward the darker fabric or the direction that will enhance the design.

A very light steam enhances the curves without stretching the fabric. Pressing, not ironing, is the secret.

There will be a few piecing seam allowance points that extend past the edge of the block. Trim them but take care to maintain the correct unfinished block size at this point of 9½" x 9½". All quilt designs in this book are based on this block size.

Refer to the quilts for a variety of designs for your blocks. The settings can be used with any of the focus blocks. Let your imagination soar.

Layer and Quilt

Layering means to place the backing wrong side up, the batting on top, and then the pieced quilt top face up over the batting. The layers are hand stitched, pinned, or machine basted about every 4". The purpose is to keep all straight and perfectly aligned while quilting. Take great care to make sure the backing is smooth and no folds or pleats are showing on the back.

Backings can be made from extra wide cotton fabric in colors to match. Fabric matching the quilt top can also be used. It usually has to be seamed to achieved the width of the quilt. Both

Curved piecing

backing and batting should be about 4" wider on all sides. This allows room for the puffing of the quilt and the trimming to a nice straight edge for binding.

Battings come in many styles and thicknesses. Very thick battings need to be hand tied every 3"–4" using strong yarn or thread. With the knots secure, you can cut the threads to a length of 1".

Quilting is the stitching that holds the three layers together. Granny Waddell would have stretched the "sandwich" on to a frame with the corners resting on the tops of four chairs and had her quilting friends join her in stitching. These gatherings were known as quilting bees. As children played under the frame, lessons for life were heard as the quilters discussed the issues of the day. Hand quilting designs came from paper-cut snowflakes, plates, cookie cutters, or custom hand-drawn images. Today, quilting stencils are plentiful for marking the images and quilting is often done using hand-guided machines. Whatever method you choose, it is what makes the quilt complete and adds greatly to the reason that quilts are special. It is important to note that instructions for quilting of all types is readily available in local quilt shops and through videos on the Internet.

Binding and Label

Binding is used to finish the edge of the quilt. It is usually made of cotton fabric that was used in the quilt, cut into 2½" strips. They are sewn end-to-end to equal the length of all

four sides of the quilt plus about 12" for corner turning. As with quilting, there are multiple ways to sew bindings. Traditionally, it is sewn to the top edge of the quilt and turned to the back and hand stitched in place, covering the raw edges. Today, many are all machine sewn and some with decorative stitching. If the quilt edge is straight, the fabric strips may be cut from straight or cross grain of the fabric. If the edge is curved, cut strips on the bias. Again, it is important to note that instructions for bindings are available in quilt shops and through videos on the Internet.

It is very important for you to make a label to attach to the back of your quilt. It should indicate who made the quilt, the date, and for whom it was made. Permanent markers such as Pilot pens can be used or a computer generated label using photo fabric available at most quilt shops.

The Most Important Thing

Quilts made for ourselves and for those we love take on a special meaning, more than just keeping us warm. It's the time and the desire to give that makes them so special. It is important to keep the reason for quilting alive and well. It connects generations for years to come and keeps us all close to each other. Whatever method suits you best is just fine. Your best effort is good enough. With each finished quilt you will improve. Keep up the good work and your family, as I with my great-grandmother, will be blessed.

THE PATTERNS

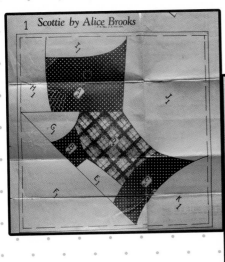

1930s

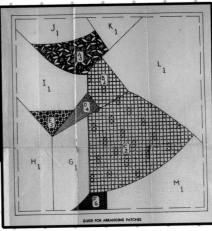

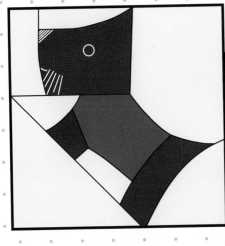

2016

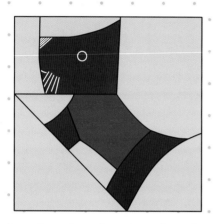

Making the Templates

Follow the general instructions for your method of choice—hand or machine piecing—and transfer the templates (pp. 16–19) to template plastic or heavy paper.

Cutting Instructions

Lay out the fabric in a single layer with the wrong side of the fabric facing up.

Place the template right-side down on the wrong side of the fabrics chosen for each piece of the block. Note the straight-of-grain arrows and align along the straight grain of the fabric. This is an important step to provide ease for curved seam piecing.

Draw around each template. Identify the wrong side of the fabric on each piece, especially if using solid material. It's easy to reverse them so they will not fit into the block. Carefully cut out each piece on the drawn line.

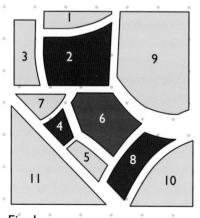

Fig. 1

Identify the Piecing Order

Arrange the pieces to see the piecing order and to ensure the correct position of each one (fig. 1). *Note: # 10 template is easy to reverse if cut from solid fabric.*

Piecing the Scottie Dog Block

Note the concave curves and the convex curves of each piece. Follow the general piecing instructions (pp. 10–11) and sew them together. Keep the edges evenly aligned. Identifying the centers of each and stopping and starting at the quarter-inch corner will ensure a good fit. Never sew into the seam allowance. Finger press seams toward the darker fabric.

Unit 1

Stitch #1 to #2 and then to #3 (figs. 2a and b).

Unit 2

Stitch #4 to #5 and then to #6 (figs. 3a, b and c).

Stitch to #7 and to #8 (figs. 4a and b).

Unit 3

Stitch Unit 1 to unit 2 (fig. 5).

Stitch #9 and #10 (fig. 6).

Stitch #11 to complete the stitching (fig. 7).

Finishing the Scottie Dog Block

Press and carefully trim the seam extensions from sides of the block. It should measure 9½" x 9½" so that the setting blocks fit (fig. 8). Refer to the general instructions for embroidery suggestions (p. 9).

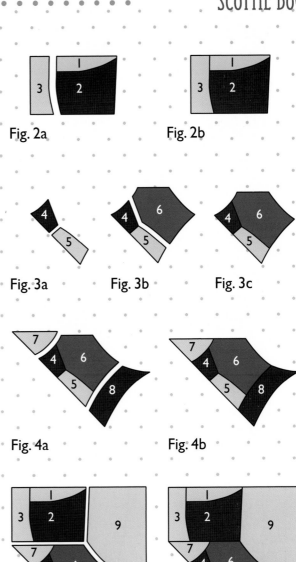

Fig. 2a　　　Fig. 2b

Fig. 3a　　Fig. 3b　　Fig. 3c

Fig. 4a　　　Fig. 4b

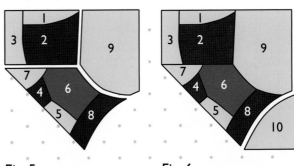

Fig. 5　　　Fig. 6

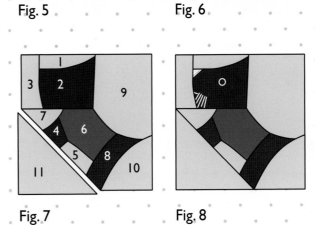

Fig. 7　　　Fig. 8

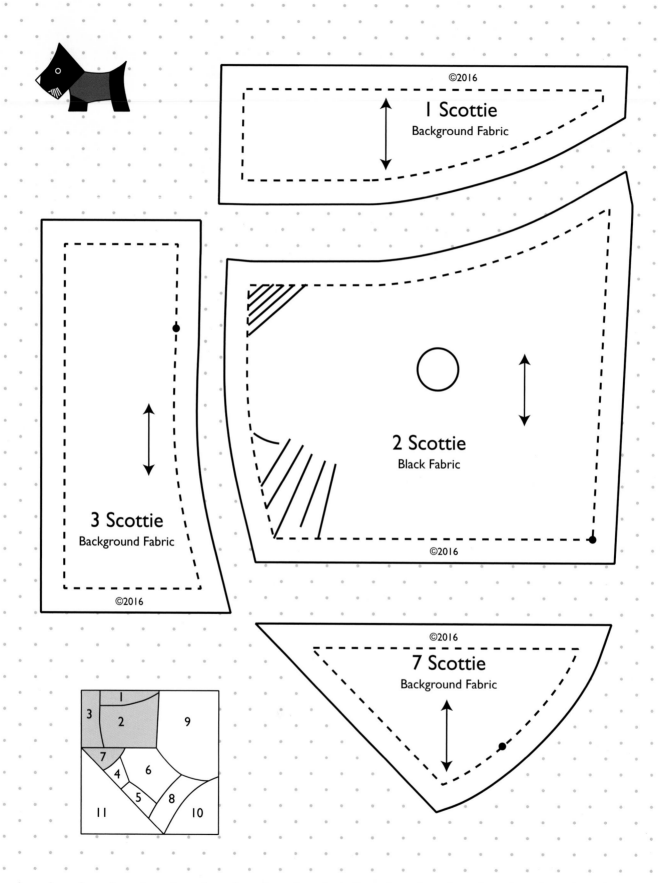

©2016

1 Scottie
Background Fabric

2 Scottie
Black Fabric

©2016

3 Scottie
Background Fabric

©2016

©2016

7 Scottie
Background Fabric

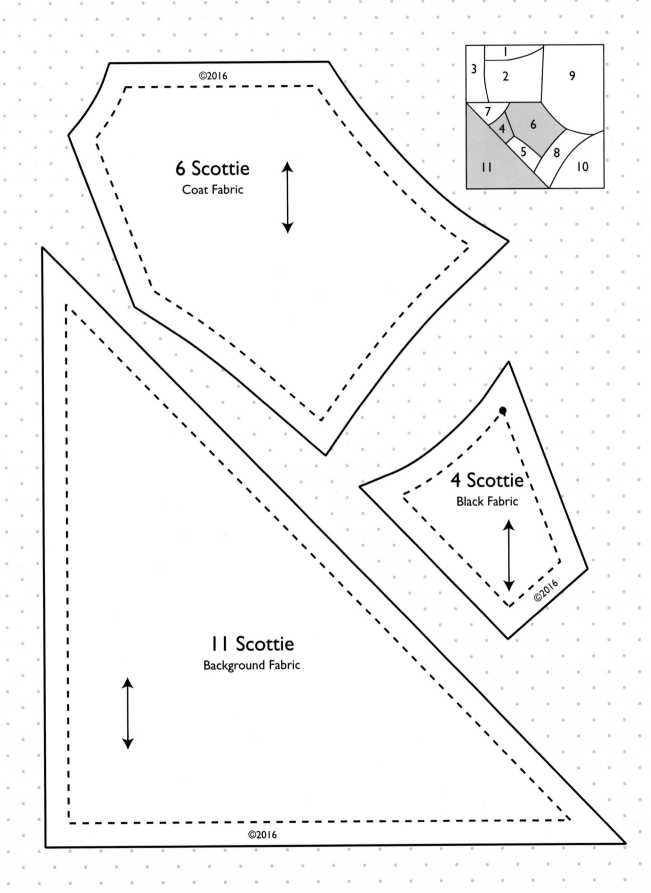

©2016

6 Scottie
Coat Fabric

4 Scottie
Black Fabric

©2016

11 Scottie
Background Fabric

©2016

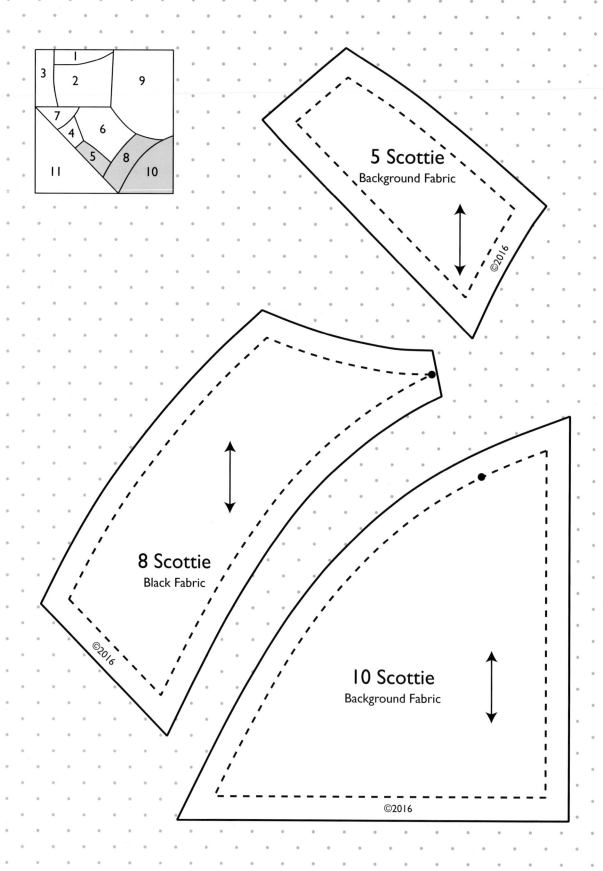

5 Scottie
Background Fabric
©2016

8 Scottie
Black Fabric
©2016

10 Scottie
Background Fabric
©2016

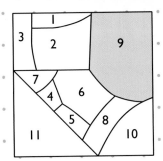

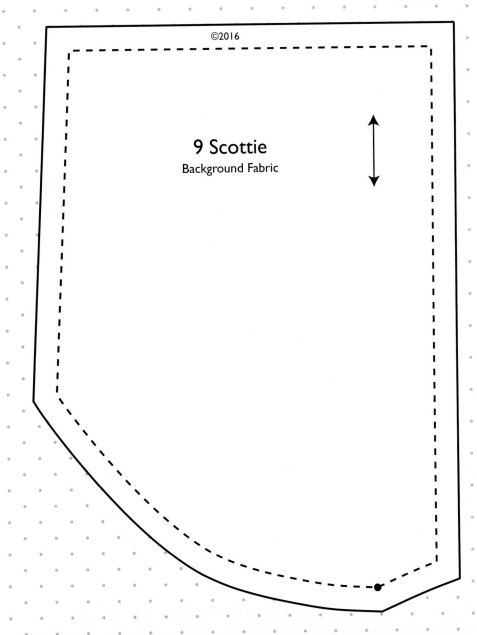

©2016

9 Scottie
Background Fabric

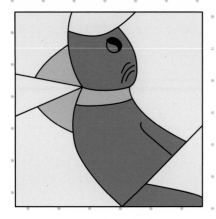

Making the Templates

Follow the general instructions for your method of choice—hand or machine piecing—and transfer the templates (pp. 22–25) to template plastic or heavy paper.

Cutting Instructions

Lay out the fabric in a single layer with the wrong side of the fabric facing up.

Place the template right-side down on the wrong side of the fabrics chosen for each piece of the block. Note the straight-of-grain arrows and align along the straight grain of the fabric. This is an important step to provide ease for curved seam piecing.

Draw around each template. Identify the wrong side of the fabric on each piece, especially if using solid material. It's easy to reverse them so they will not fit into the block. Carefully cut out each piece on the drawn line.

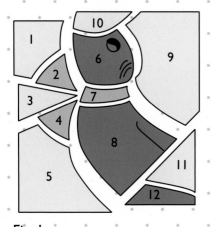

Fig. 1

Identify the Piecing Order

Arrange the pieces to see the piecing order and to ensure the correct position of each one (fig. 1). *Note: #2 and #4 template is easy to reverse if cut from solid fabric.*

Piecing the Calico Cat Block

Note the concave curves and the convex curves of each piece. Follow the general piecing instructions (pp. 10–11) and sew them together. Keep the edges evenly aligned. Identifying the centers of each and stopping and starting at the quarter-inch corner will ensure a good fit. Never sew into the seam allowance. Finger press seams toward the darker fabric.

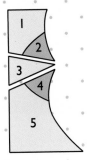
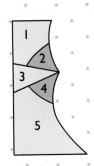

Fig. 2a   Fig. 2b   Fig. 2c

Unit 1

Stitch #1 to #2 (fig. 2a).

Stitch #4 to #5 (fig. 2b), then stitch #3 in between (fig. 2c).

Unit 2

Stitch #6 to #7 to #8 (fig. 3).

Stitch to #9 (fig. 4), and then to #10 (fig. 5).

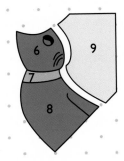

Fig. 3   Fig. 4

Unit 3

Stitch #11 to #12 (fig. 6).

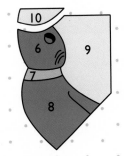

Fig. 5   Fig. 6

Unit 4

Stitch Unit 1 to Unit 2 then add #3 (fig. 7).

Finishing the Calico Cat Block

Press and carefully trim the seam extensions from sides of the block. It should measure 9½" x 9½" so that the setting blocks fit (fig. 8). Refer to the general instructions for embroidery suggestions (p. 9).

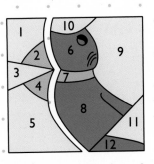
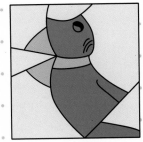

Fig. 7   Fig. 8

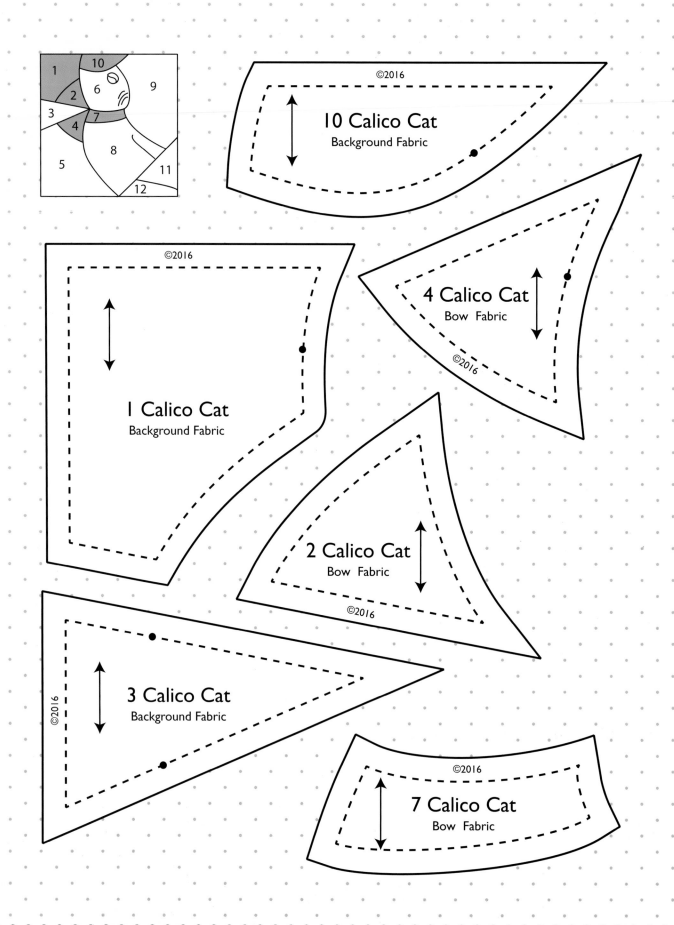

10 Calico Cat
Background Fabric
©2016

4 Calico Cat
Bow Fabric
©2016

1 Calico Cat
Background Fabric
©2016

2 Calico Cat
Bow Fabric
©2016

3 Calico Cat
Background Fabric
©2016

7 Calico Cat
Bow Fabric
©2016

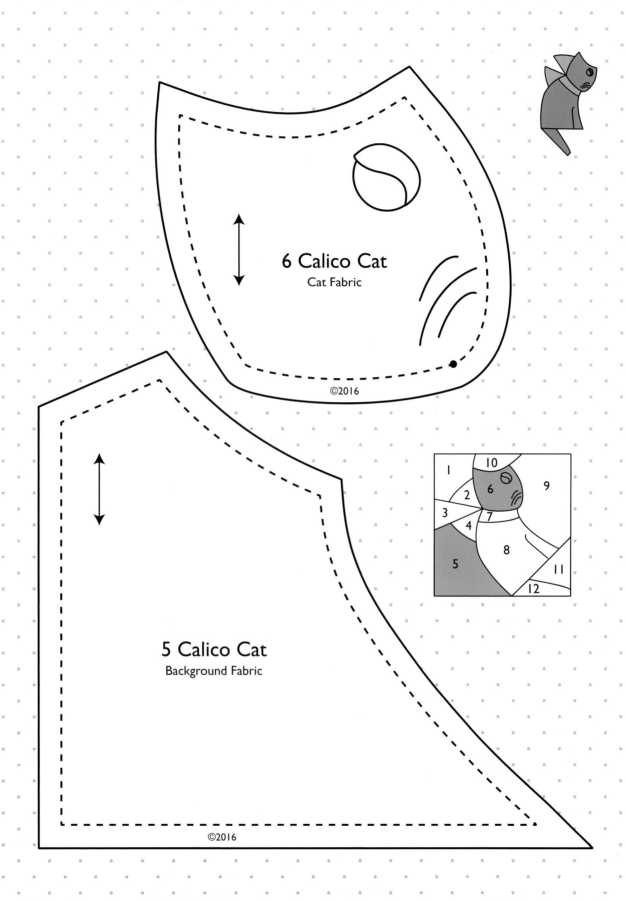

6 Calico Cat
Cat Fabric

©2016

5 Calico Cat
Background Fabric

©2016

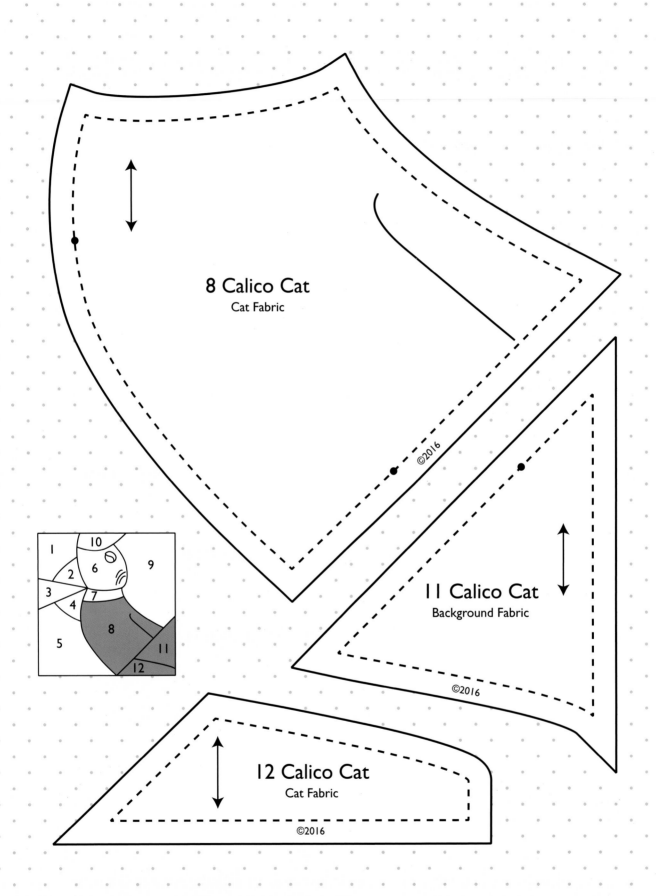

8 Calico Cat
Cat Fabric

©2016

11 Calico Cat
Background Fabric

©2016

12 Calico Cat
Cat Fabric

©2016

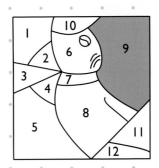

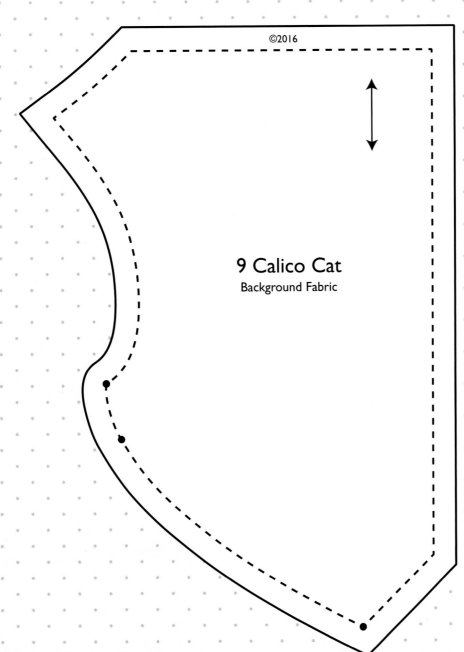

©2016

9 Calico Cat
Background Fabric

Making the Templates

Follow the general instructions for your method of choice—hand or machine piecing—and transfer the templates (pp. 28–31) to template plastic or heavy paper.

Cutting Instructions

Lay out the fabric in a single layer with the wrong side of the fabric facing up.

Place the template right-side down on the wrong side of the fabrics chosen for each piece of the block. Note the straight-of-grain arrows and align along the straight grain of the fabric. This is an important step to provide ease for curved seam piecing.

Draw around each template. Identify the wrong side of the fabric on each piece, especially if using solid material. It's easy to reverse them so they will not fit into the block. Carefully cut out each piece on the drawn line.

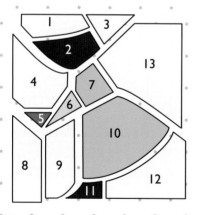

Fig. I

Identify the Piecing Order

Arrange the pieces to see the piecing order and to ensure the correct position of each one (fig. 1). *Note: #10 template is easy to reverse if cut from solid fabric.*

Piecing the Mighty Pretty Girl Block

Note the concave curves and the convex curves of each piece. Follow the general piecing instructions (pp. 10–11) and sew them together. Keep the edges evenly aligned. Identifying the centers of each and stopping and starting at the quarter-inch corner will ensure a good fit. Never sew into the seam allowance. Finger press seams toward the darker fabric.

Unit 1

Stitch #1 to #2 (fig. 2a).

Stitch to #3 (fig. 2b).

Unit 2

Stitch #4 to #5 (figs. 3a and 3b).

Stitch #6 to #7 (figs. 4a and 4b).

Stitch both to Unit 1 (fig. 5).

Unit 3

Stitch #8 to #9 to #10 (fig. 6).

Stitch to Unit 2 (fig. 7).

Unit 4

Sew #11 to #12 (fig. 7).

Sew to Unit 3 (fig. 8).

Finish stitching #13 (fig. 9).

Refer to the general instructions to finish with hand embroidery, fabric paint, or a machine embroidered design (fig. 10).

Press and carefully trim the seam extensions from the sides. It should measure 9½" x 9½" so that the setting blocks fit.

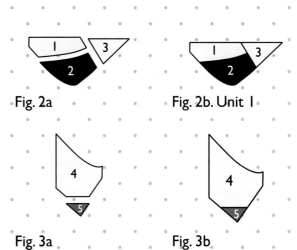

Fig. 2a

Fig. 2b. Unit 1

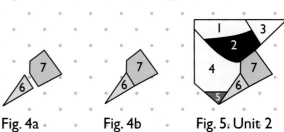

Fig. 3a

Fig. 3b

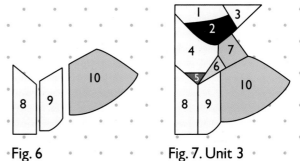

Fig. 4a   Fig. 4b   Fig. 5. Unit 2

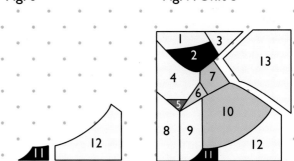

Fig. 6

Fig. 7. Unit 3

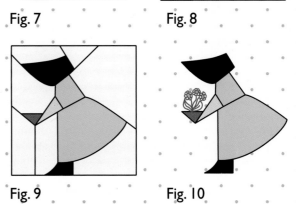

Fig. 7

Fig. 8

Fig. 9

Fig. 10

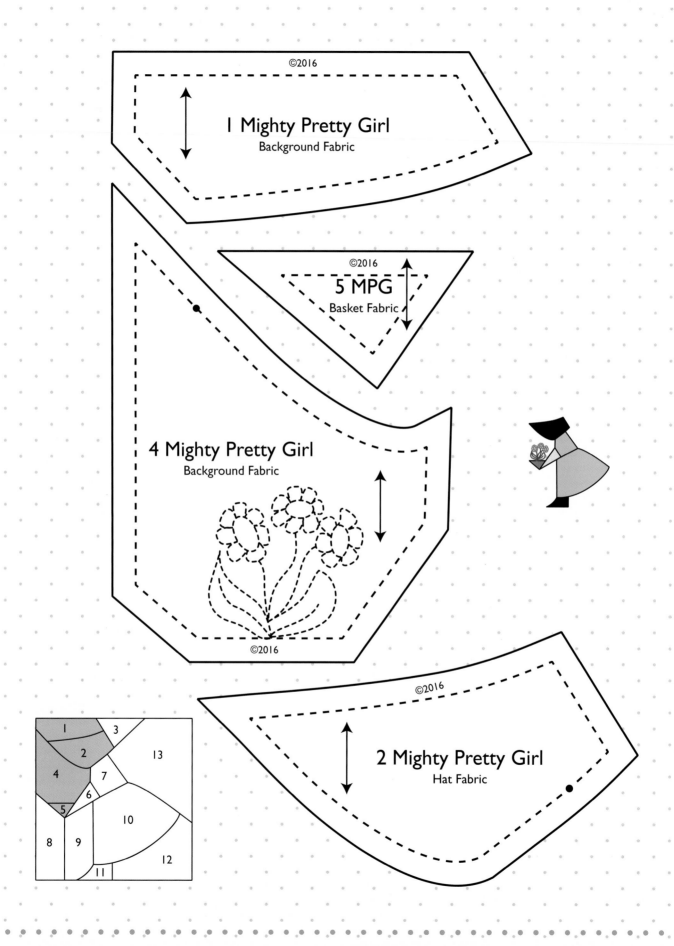

©2016

1 Mighty Pretty Girl
Background Fabric

©2016

5 MPG
Basket Fabric

4 Mighty Pretty Girl
Background Fabric

©2016

©2016

2 Mighty Pretty Girl
Hat Fabric

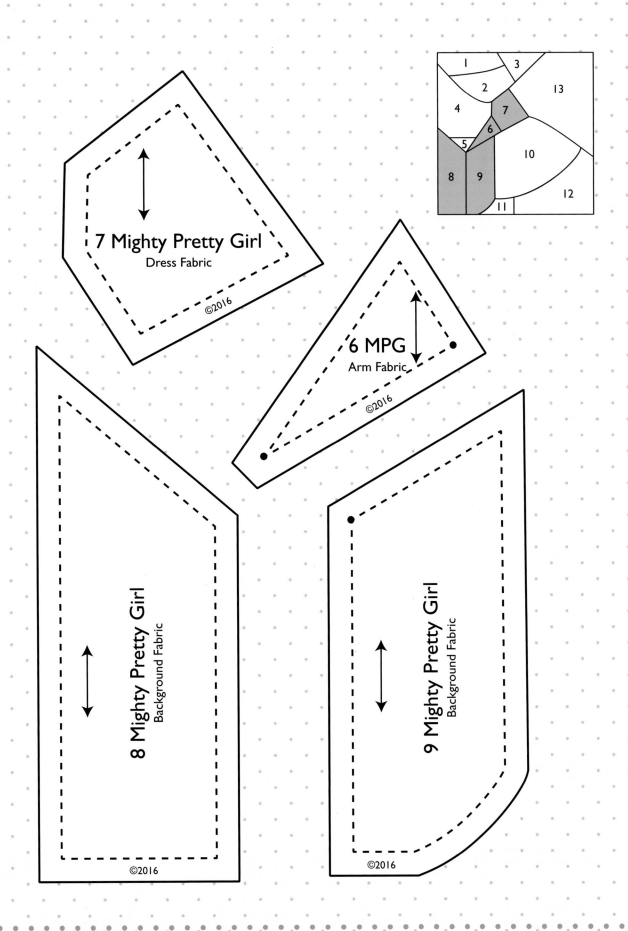

7 Mighty Pretty Girl
Dress Fabric
©2016

6 MPG
Arm Fabric
©2016

8 Mighty Pretty Girl
Background Fabric
©2016

9 Mighty Pretty Girl
Background Fabric
©2016

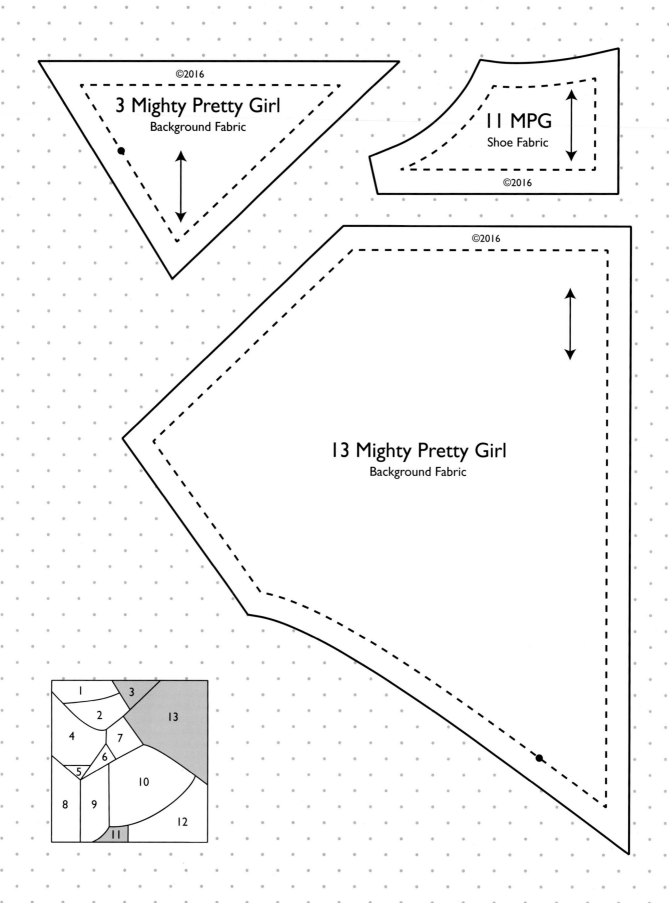

©2016

3 Mighty Pretty Girl
Background Fabric

11 MPG
Shoe Fabric

©2016

©2016

13 Mighty Pretty Girl
Background Fabric

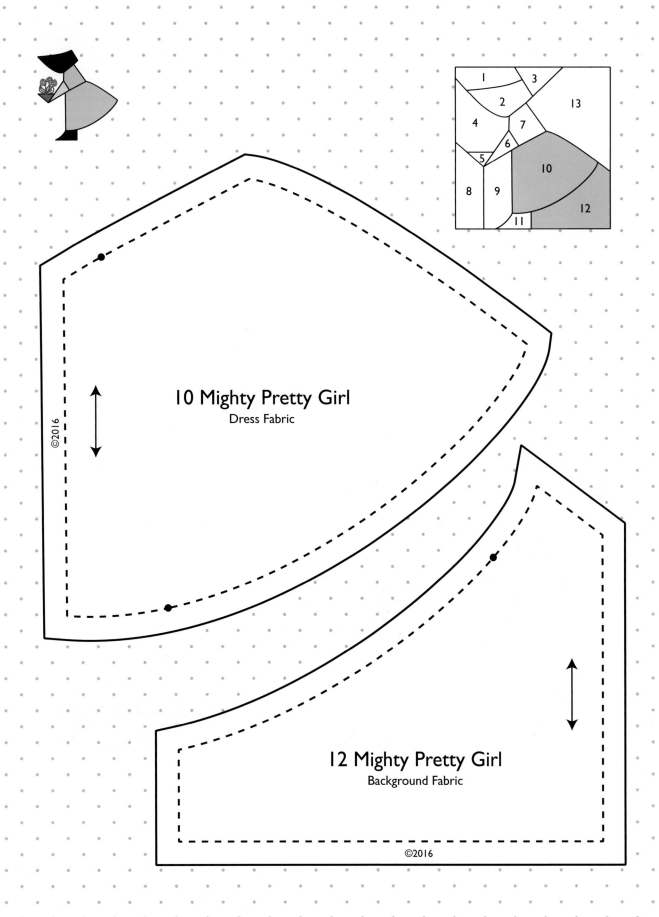

10 Mighty Pretty Girl
Dress Fabric

©2016

12 Mighty Pretty Girl
Background Fabric

©2016

THE QUILTS

The quilt patterns offer a variety of settings. When made from fabrics either from the era when the patterns were designed (the 1930s) or from modern fabrics (such as batiks) they provide quilt projects for you to make for years to come.

There is an additional advantage in that all settings can use any of the three focus blocks or a combination of the three. The setting blocks have been drafted to fit the 9" x 9" finished size of the focus blocks (9½" x 9½" as pieced).

42

48

51

54

57

60

SCOTTIE RIBBONS, 42" x 42", made by the author.
Machine quilted by Pat Roche, Gilbert, Arizona

SCOTTIE RIBBONS

Finished Quilt: 42" x 42"
Finished Block Size: 9" x 9"

Fabric Requirements

- ¼ yard each of 4 red fabrics
- ⅝ yard of black fabric includes border and Scottie dogs
- ⅝ yard additional red fabric includes side squares and binding
- 1 yard background fabric
- ¼ yard coats for Scottie dogs
- 46" x 46" for backing fabric
- 2¾ yards for batting
- Cream color embroidery thread

Cutting Instructions
Step 1

Red fabrics
> Cut (4) each 1¼" x 40" strips.

Additional red fabric
> Cut (4) 3½" x 40" strips.

Black fabric
> Cut (2) 3½" x 40½" strips .

Step 2

Sew strips into 2 different stratas. Then following the instructions in figs. 1 and 2 below cut into units.

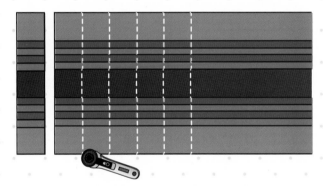

Fig. 1. Sew (1) strata 15½" wide. Cut into (6) units 3½" x 15½"

Fig. 2. Sew (1) strata 9½" wide. Cut into (10) units 3½" x 9½"

Design Idea

Calico Cats and Mighty Pretty Girls blocks can be used too.

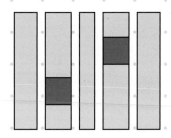

Fig. 3

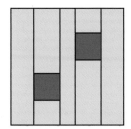

Fig. 4

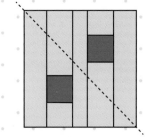

Fig. 5

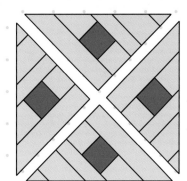

Fig. 6

Step 3

Background fabric

Cut (2) 11" x 11" squares.

Cut (3) 3½" x 40" strips.

Then cut the following:

(4) 4½" x 8½"

(4) 3½" x 4½"

(4) 3½" x 15½"

(1) 1½" x 15½"

Red fabric

Cut (4) 3½" x 3½"

Making the Pieced Side Setting Triangles

Select the pieces cut from background fabric and the red squares (fig. 3).

Sew 2 blocks as shown (fig. 4).

Each block should measure 15½" x 15½".

Cut apart diagonally between the red squares (fig. 5) to form 4 side setting triangle units (fig. 6).

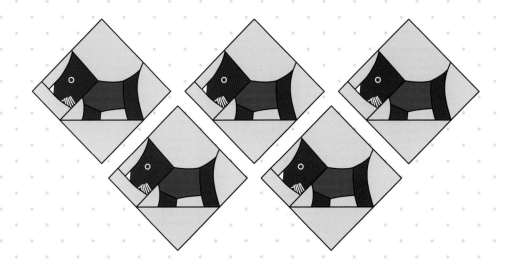

Fig. 7

Making the Scottie Dogs

Refer to the Scottie Dog pattern (pp. 16–19) and make 5 Scottie blocks (fig. 7).

Piecing the Quilt

Select the ribbon units, Scotties, and side setting triangles.

Arrange them as shown into blocks.

Sew blocks together in rows. Sew the rows together (fig. 8).

Notice that the side triangles extend beyond the blocks.

Select the 2 background squares. Cut apart diagonally to form 4 corner triangles (fig. 9). Sew to corners (fig. 10).

Fig. 9

Finishing the Quilt

Cut (4) 2½" x 40" strips of black and sew the border around the quilt (fig. 11).

Layer with batting and backing. Hand or machine quilt.

Cut binding from additional red fabric (4) 2½" x 40". Add to the quilt.

Fig. 8

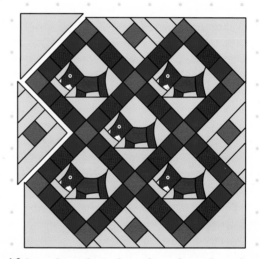

Fig. 10

Fig. 11

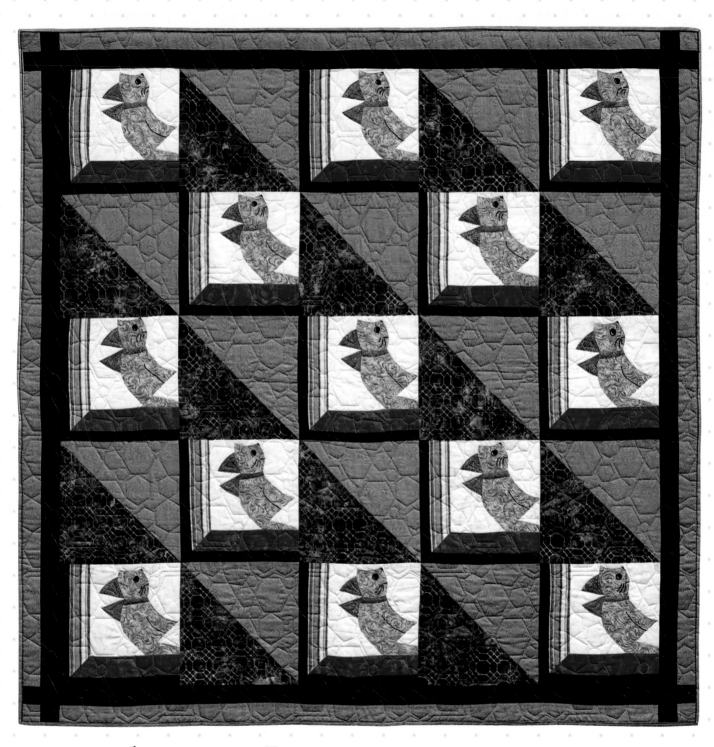

Cats in the Attic, 68" x 68", made by the author.
Machine quilted by Pat Roche, Gilbert, Arizona

CATS IN THE ATTIC

Finished Quilt: 68" x 68"
Finished Block Size: 12" x 12"

Fabric Requirements

- 1⅜ yards light brown fabric
- 1⅝ yards dark brown includes binding
- 1¼ yards black fabric
- 1 yard Calico Cat background fabric
- ¾ yard Calico Cat fabric
- ¼ yard bow fabric
- ¾ yard light striped fabric
- ¾ yard dark red fabric
- 4⅜ yards for backing fabric
- 76" x 76" for batting
- Embroidery Thread

Making the Setting Triangle Blocks

Cut (6) each of the light and dark brown fabrics 12⅞" x 12⅞".

Cut each diagonally and sew to form 12 squares (fig. 1).

Each block should measure 12½" x 12½".

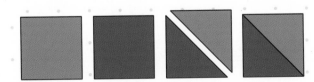

Fig. 1

Making the Calico Cats

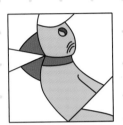

Refer to the Calico Cat pattern (pp. 22–25) and make 13 Calico Cat blocks.

Cutting the Attic Window Frame

Cut (13) 2½" x 11" frame side from light striped fabric.

Cut (13) 2½" x 11" frame bottom from dark red fabric, measure and trim a 45-degree angle as shown from each (fig. 2). *Note: Angles are mirror image of each other.*

Cut (13) 1½" x 11½" bottom frame black fabric (fig. 3).

Cut (13) 1½" x 12½" side frame black fabric (fig. 3).

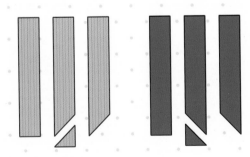

Fig. 2

Fig. 3

Fig. 4

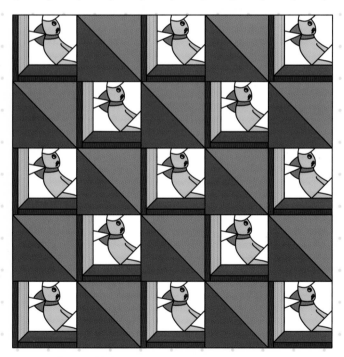

Fig. 5

Fig. 6

Framing the Calico Cats

Arrange the framing pieces and sew as shown (fig. 5).

Repeat to make 13 Calico Cat blocks.

Each block should measure 12½" x 12½".

Piecing the Blocks

Arrange blocks, beginning with a Calico Cat block and alternating with setting blocks, 5 across x 5 down. Sew together (fig. 6).

Making the Pieced Borders

Cut (8) 2½" x 40" strips from black fabric.

Cut (8) 2½" x 40" strips from light brown fabric.

Sew black strips end-to-end to form a long strip approx. 264" long.

Repeat to sew the light brown fabric.

Sew the long strips together as shown (fig. 4). Width should be 4½".

Adding the Borders

Measure the length and width of the quilt. It should measure 60½" x 60½".

Select the pieced border unit.

Cut (4) 60½" lengths (or your width and length measurement) (fig. 7).

Make 4 corner squares from remaining border unit (fig. 8).

Slice across 2½".

Cut black 2½" x 4½".

Sew together to make a square.

Squares should measure 4½" x 4½".

Sew side borders onto the quilt.

Sew corner blocks to each side of the top and the bottom border unit.

Sew to the quilt (fig. 9).

Finishing the Quilt

Layer with batting and backing. Hand or machine quilt.

Cut binding from dark brown fabric. (5) 2½" x 40" strips.

Join end-to-end and add to the quilt.

Fig. 7

Fig. 8

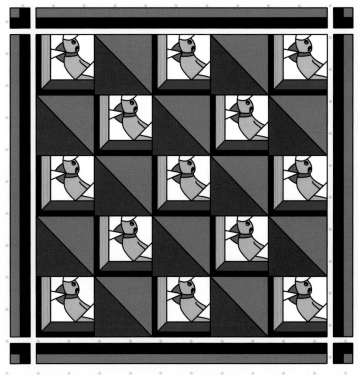

Fig. 9

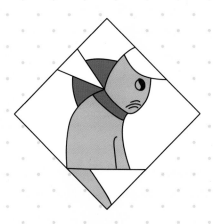

Best Friends Forever, 66" x 82", made by the author. Machine quilted by Pat Roche, Gilbert, Arizona

Finished Quilt: 66" x 82"
Finished Block Size: 12" x 12"

Fabric Requirements

- 1¼ yard green frames and binding
  Note: Pieces need to be cut from the length of the fabric not across. Some of the cuts are very long.

- 1 yard dark gray frame shadows

- 2¾ yards light gray background fabric
  Note: Cut from the length of fabric.

- ¼ yard bow fabric

Scottie Dog, Calico Cat, A Mighty Pretty Girl 4 Blocks each:

- 1½ yards block background fabric
- ½ yard dog fabric
- ¼ yard dog coat fabric
- ½ yard cats fabric
- 8" x 8" cat bows fabric
- ½ yard dress fabric
- 6" x 6" for each shoes, basket, arm
- 8" x 8" hat fabric
- 70" x 86" backing fabric and batting
- Embroidery thread or fabric markers

Cutting the Frames and Borders

Green fabric

  Cut (24) 1½" x 9½"

  Cut (24) 1½" x 11½"

  Cut (1) 2½" x 25"

  Cut (1) 2½" x 44"

Dark Gray Fabric

  Cut (14) 4½" x 9"

  Cut (4) 4½" x 4½

  Cut (1) 6½" x 25"

  Cut (12) 2" x 10"

Note: Cut from the length of fabric.

Light Gray Fabric

  Cut (4) 4½" x 70½"

  Cut (2) 2½" x 54"

  Cut (2) 2½" x 74½"

  Cut (1) 6½" x 44"

  Cut (1) 5" x 44"

  Cut (12) 5½" x 2½"

  Cut (12) 4" x 2½"

  Cut (24) 2" x 2"

  Cut (1) 2" x 20"

  Cut (8) 4½" x 11"

Fig. 1. Make 12 bows
2" x 4"

Fig. 2. Make 18 bows
4" x 6"

Making the Blocks: Scottie Dog, Calico Cat and A Mighty Pretty Girl

Refer to the patterns to make 4 of each block: Scottie Dog (pp. 16–19), Calico Cat (pp. 22–25), and the A Mighty Pretty Girl (pp. 28–31).

Fig. 3

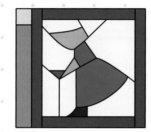

Fig. 4

Framing the Blocks

Select the green pieces and sew around blocks (fig. 3).

Select 1½" x 9½" for top and bottom.

Select 1½" x 11½" for sides.

Each block should measure 11½" x 11½"

Select 12 light gray 2" x 2" squares.
12 dark gray 2" x 10" pieces.

Sew together as shown.

Then sew to the block (fig. 4).

Each block should measure 13" x 11½".

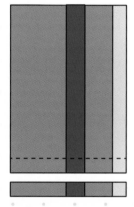

Fig. 5. Unit A 2" x 13"

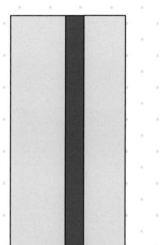

Making the Bows for the Quilt and Border

Make (12) bows 2" x 4" finished size (fig. 1).

Make (18) bows 4" x 6" finished size (fig. 2).

Follow directions on templates (p. 47).

Fig. 6. Unit B
3½" x 13"

Making the Setting Units
Unit A
Select the Dark gray 6½" x 25"

  Dark gray 3½" x 25"

  Green 2½" x 25"

  Light gray 2" x 25"

Sew the strata (fig. 5). Cut (12) 2" x 13"

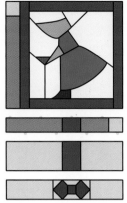

Unit B
Select the light gray 6½" x 44"

  Light gray 5" x 44"

  Green 2½" x 44"

Sew the strata (fig. 6). Cut (12) 3½" x 13"

Fig. 7

Arrange the blocks and setting units and sew them as shown (fig. 7). Make 4 of each block.

Repeat for each Block for a total of 12 Block units (fig. 8).

Making the Block Bow unit
Select the light gray 2½" x 5½" and 2½" x 4".
Make 12 small bows.

Sew together as shown.

The unit should measure 2½" x 13".

Block bow unit

Sew the Border
Select dark gray 4½" x 9" pieces and 4 large bows.

Sew alternately for top border.

Repeat for the bottom border.

Fig. 8. Make 4 of each set

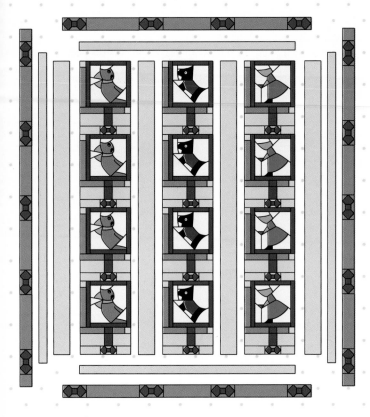

Fig. 9

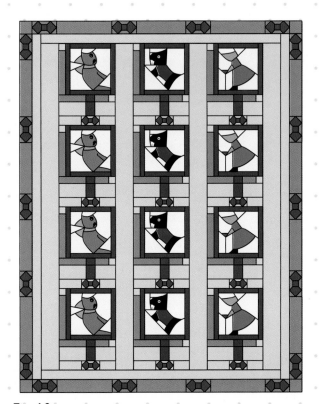

Fig. 10

Select dark gray 4½" x 9" pieces and 5 large bows.

Sew alternately for the side border.

Add a 4½" x 4½" square to each end.

Repeat for the remaining side border.

Piecing the Quilt

Measure length and width of quilt and note if adjustments are needed. (fig. 9)

Select the framed block units.

Sew each type in a row by design.

Sew the 4½" x 70½" light gray strips between the rows. The top should measure 54" x 70½".

Select 2½" x 54" strips and sew to the top and bottom of quilt.

Select 2½" x 74½" strips and sew on each side of the quilt.

Sew the top and bottom bow units to the quilt.

Sew the side bow units to each side of the quilt (fig. 10).

Finishing the Quilt

Layer with batting and backing. Hand or machine quilt.

Cut binding (6) 2½" x 44" strips from green fabric.

Join end-to-end and add to the quilt.

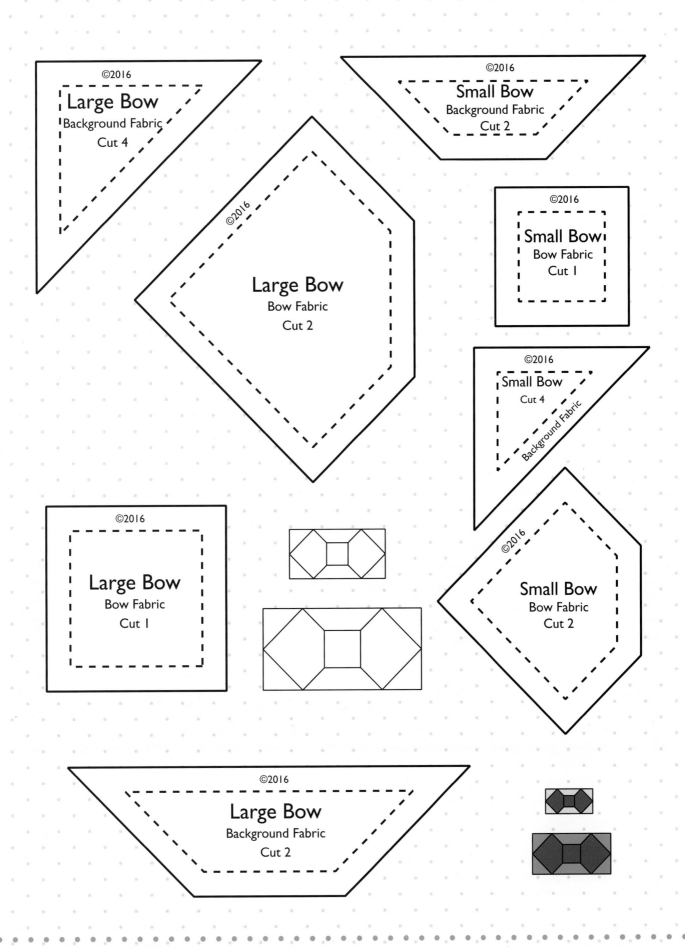

Large Bow
Background Fabric
Cut 4
©2016

Small Bow
Background Fabric
Cut 2
©2016

Large Bow
Bow Fabric
Cut 2
©2016

Small Bow
Bow Fabric
Cut 1
©2016

Small Bow
Cut 4
Background Fabric
©2016

Large Bow
Bow Fabric
Cut 1
©2016

Small Bow
Bow Fabric
Cut 2
©2016

Large Bow
Background Fabric
Cut 2
©2016

EASY GOING, 58" x 58", made by the author.
Machine quilted by Pat Roche, Gilbert, Arizona

Easy Going

Finished Quilt: 58" x 58"
Finished Block Size: 9" x 9"

Fabric Requirements

5 Scottie Dogs, 4 Calico Cats,
4 A Mighty Pretty Girls

- 1½ yards background fabric
- ½ yard dogs fabric
- ½ yard dogs coat fabric
- ½ yard cats fabric
- 8" x 8" cat bows fabric
- ½ yard dress fabric
- 6" x 6" each for shoes, baskets, and arms
- 8" x 8" hat fabric
- Embroidery thread or fabric pens

12 Snowball Blocks

- 1⅔ yards print fabric includes the border and binding
- 1½ yard dark blue accent fabric
- 3⅞ yards backing fabric
- 66" x 66" batting

Making the Blocks

Refer to the patterns to make 5 Scottie Dog (pp. 16–19), 4 Calico Cat (pp. 22–25), and 4 A Mighty Pretty Girl (pp. 28–31) blocks.

Making the Snowball Blocks

Cut (12) 9½" x 9½" squares from print fabric. Cut from length of fabric to preserve the length for borders.

Cut (48) 3½" x 3½" squares from dark blue accent fabric. Cut from length of fabric to preserve the length for borders.

Fold each dark blue square diagonally to form triangle.

Open and follow the press line to sew on each corner. Trim. Fold back (fig. 1).

Make 12.

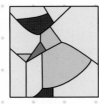

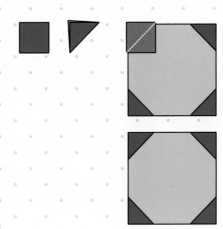

Fig. 1

Anne Dutton ∿ *VINTAGE* **Quilt Treasures** 1930s Revisited

49 ∿

Fig. 2

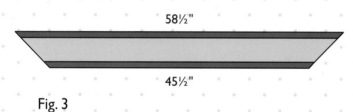

58½"

45½"

Fig. 3

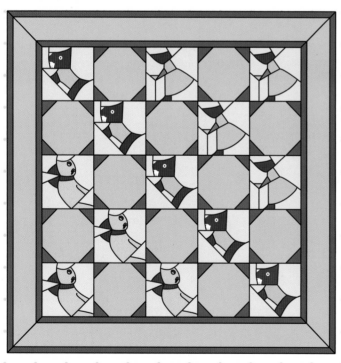

Fig. 4

Piece the Quilt

Sew the blocks alternately as shown (fig. 2).

Border

Cut (12) 1½" x 45½" strips from dark blue fabric.

Cut (6) 4½" x 58½" strips from print fabric.

Sew each set of 6 strips end-to-end.

Then sew a combination as shown (fig. 3).

Cut into (4) lengths 58½" long.

Trim 45-degree angle on each end as shown (fig. 3).

Sew around quilt and stitch out to the corners (fig. 4).

Finishing the Quilt

Layer with batting and backing and quilt.

Cut (5) 2½" x 40" strips from the print fabric for binding.

Join end-to-end and add to the quilt.

 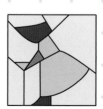

SCOTTIE, 82" x 82", made by the author.
Machine quilted by Pat Roche, Gilbert, Arizona

Finished Quilt: 82" x 82"
Finished Block Size: 16" x 16"

Fabric Requirements

- 2¾ yards background fabric includes binding
- 1½ yards black fabric includes Scotties
- 1 yards gold fabric
- 1¼ yards green fabric
- 1¼ yards red fabric
- ½ yard Scotties coat fabric
- 5⅛ yards backing fabric
- 87" x 87" Batting
- Embroidery thread

Fig. 1. Make 16.

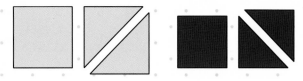

Fig. 2. Cut to make 32 triangles of each fabric.

1½"
9½"

Fig. 3. Cut a (32) 1½" x 9½" gold strips

Make (16) Scottie Dogs

Refer to pattern (pp. 16–19) and make 16 Scotties Dogs (fig. 1).

Piecing the Blocks

Corners: background fabric

Cut (3) 6⅞" x 40" strips. Then cut (16) 6⅞" x 6⅞" squares.

Cut diagonally to form (32) triangles (fig. 2).

Pieced corners: black with gold

Cut (3) 5⅞" x 40" black strips. Then cut (16) 5⅞" x 5⅞" squares.

Cut diagonally to form (32) triangles (fig. 2).

Cut (8) 1½" x 40" gold strips. Then cut (32) 1½" x 9⅞" gold strips (fig. 3).

Sew gold strips to black triangles and trim the ends at an angle (fig.4).

Adding the Corners to Scottie

Sew corners as shown (fig. 5). Make (8) of each type

Each block should measure 12½" x 12½"

Bordering the Blocks

Green fabric

Cut (6) 2½" x 40" strips. Then cut (16) 2½" x 12½" strips.

Cut (8) 2½" x 44" strips. Then cut (16) 2½" x 16½".

Red fabric

Cut (6) 2½" x 40" strips. Then cut (16) 2½" x 12½".

Cut (8) 2½" x 40" strips. Then cut (16) 2½" x 16½".

Sew to the sides, then to the top and bottom of each block (fig. 6).

Notice the dark and light corners for placement.

Setting the Blocks Together

Background fabric

Cut (14) 3½" x 40" strips. Then cut (28) 3½" x 17¼".

Gold fabric

Cut (3) 3½" x 40½" strips. Then cut (25) 3½" x 3½" squares

Sew the setting pieces and the blocks in rows (fig. 7). Notice dark and light corners for placement.

Sew the Gold squares between background pieces to make (5) rows (fig. 8).

Sew toward the sides and between the rows (fig. 9).

Finishing the Quilt

Layer with backing and batting and hand or machine quilt.

Cut (8) 2½" x 40" strips.

Sew end-to-end to form the binding and and add to the quilt.

Fig. 4

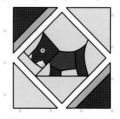

Fig. 5

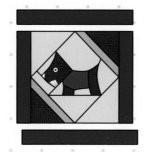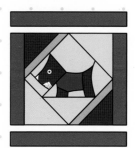

Fig. 6

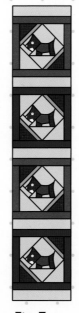

Fig. 7   Fig. 9

Fig. 8

SCRAPPY GIRLS, 38" x 56", made by the author.
Machine quilted by Pat Roche, Gilbert, Arizona

SCRAPPY GIRL

Finished Quilt: 38" x 56"
Finished Block Size: 9" x 9"

Fabric Requirements

Select fabric from your stash

- ⅛ yard of 6 different colors of fabric or (12) strips 2⅜" x 21"
- 1⅛ yards black fabric
- 1⅔ yards background fabric includes 7 A Mighty Pretty Girl blocks
- 1¾ yards stripe fabric (4 repeats of stripe design). Cut from length into 4 identical designs. Cut binding strips from inbetween design
- 12" x 12" hat fabric
- 8" x 8" of each fabric for shoes, basket, and arms
- 3¾ yards backing fabric
- 46" x 64" backing fabric and batting
  Note: depends on width of the border stripe

Making the A Mighty Pretty Girls

Refer to the pattern (pp. 28–31) and make 7 A Mighty Pretty Girl Blocks.

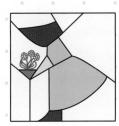

Fig. 1. Make 7.

Making the Pieced Blocks

Cut (12) strips in a variety of colors 2⅜" x 21"

Cut (6) black strips 2⅜" x 40". Then cut (9) 2⅜" x 20"

Cut (2) background strips 2⅜" x 40". Then cut (4) 2⅜" x 20"

Sew (5) Sets in order as shown (A–E, fig. 2, p. 56).

Black and background need to be placed in specific order.

The 12 colors are random.

Cut across each Strata 2⅜" to yield (8) units from each strata. (A–E, fig. 2, p. 56).

Sew the units to make 8 blocks (fig. 3, p. 56).

Sewing the Quilt

Sew pieced blocks alternately with the Girls (fig. 4, p. 56).

Sew the stripe border.

Finishing the Quilt

Layer with batting and backing and quilt.

Cut (3) 2½" x 40" strips for the binding.

Join end-to-end and add to the quilt.

A   B   C   D   E

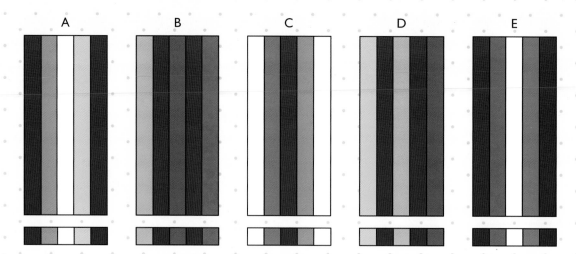

Fig. 2

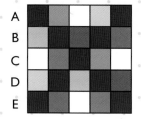

A
B
C
D
E

Fig. 3

Fig. 4

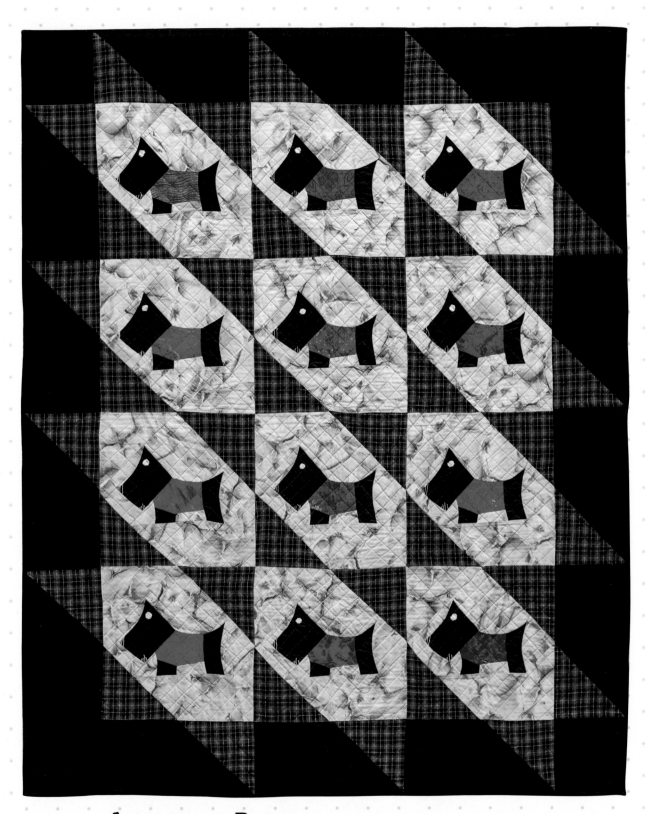

SCOTTIE IN PLAID, 48" x 60", made and machine quilted by the author.

SCOTTIE IN PLAID

Finished Quilt: 48" x 60"
Finished Block Size: 12" x 12"

Fabric Requirements

- 2 yards light background fabric
- 2⅔ yards black fabric includes Scotties and binding
- 1⅓ yards plaid fabric
- ⅓ yard Scottie coats fabric
- 4 yards backing fabric
- 56" x 68" batting
- Embroidery thread

Making the Scottie Dogs

Refer to the patterns (pp. 16–19) and make 12 Scotties (fig. 1).

Fig. 1. Make 12.

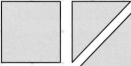

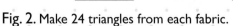

Fig. 2. Make 24 triangles from each fabric.

Making the Blocks

Cut 3 background strips 6⅞" x 40". Then cut 12 squares 6⅞" x 6⅞".

Cut in half diagonally to form 24 triangles (fig. 2).

Cut 4 plaid strips 6⅞" x 40". Then cut 19 squares 6⅞" x 6⅞".

Cut in half diagonally to form 38 triangles (fig. 2).

Sew 2 plaid and 2 background triangles on opposite sides of the Scotties, as shown (fig. 3).

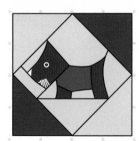

Fig. 3

Cut 2 black strips 6⅞" x 40". Then cut 7 squares 6⅞" x 6⅞".

Cut in half diagonally to form 14 triangles (fig. 4).

Sew 1 plaid and 1 black triangle to make 14 half-square triangles (fig. 4).

Cut 3 black strips 6½" x 40". Then cut 18 squares 6½" x 6½" (fig. 5).

Set the blocks, side squares, and corners as shown (fig. 6).

Finishing the Quilt

Layer with batting and backing and quilt.

Cut (5) 2½" x 44" strips.

Cut Plaid (5) 2½" x 40" strips for the binding. Join end-to-end and add to the quilt.

Fig. 4. Make 14 half-square triangles.

Fig. 5. Make 18 squares.

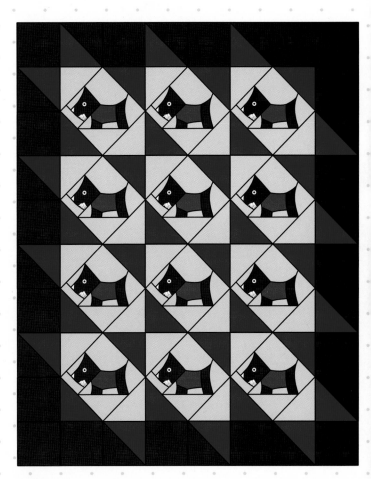

Fig. 6

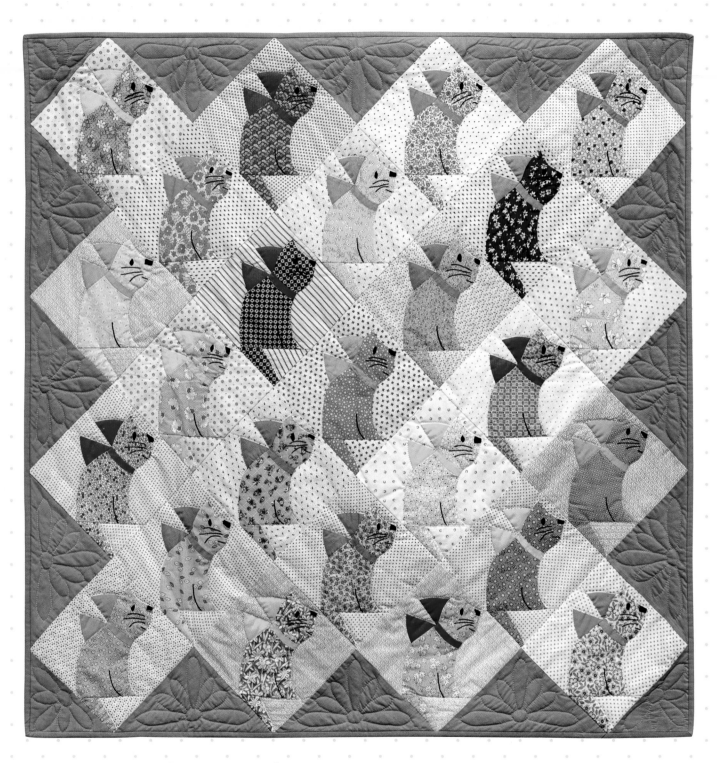

SCRAPPY CAT, 50" x 50", made by the author.
Hand quilted by Dorothy Dodds, Tempe, Arizona

Scrappy Cat

Finished Quilt: 50" x 50"
Finished Block Size: 12" x 12"

Fabric Requirements

- (25) 11" x 11" scrap fabrics for cats
- (25) 6" x 6" scrap fabrics for bows
- (25) 12" x 12" scrap fabric for backgrounds
- 1½ yards setting triangles fabric includes corners and binding
- 3¾ yards backing fabric
- 64" x 64" batting
- Embroidery Thread

Making the Cats

Refer to the pattern (pp. 22–25) and make 25 Calico Cats (fig. 1).

Fig. 1. Make 25.

Background Side Setting Triangles

Cut 2 background strips 14" x 40". Then cut (3) 14" x 14".

Cut diagonally twice to make side triangles (fig. 2).

Note: Long side will be on straight of grain.

Background Corner Triangles

Cut (2) background strips 7" x 7".

Cut diagonally into triangles (fig. 3).

Note: The corner will be on straight-of-grain.

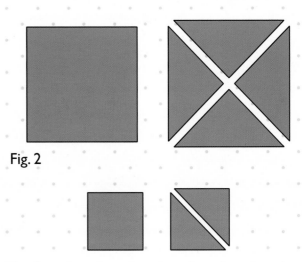

Fig. 2

Fig. 3

Fig. 4

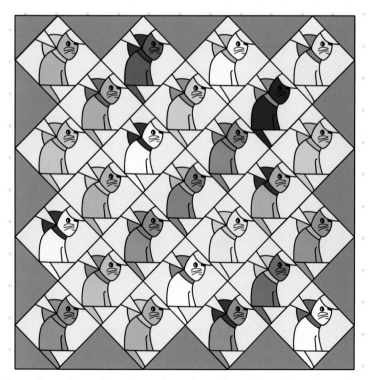

Fig. 5

Piecing the Quilt

Lay out the blocks and setting triangles in diagonal rows.

Start at the arrow and sew in rows (fig. 4).

Then sew the rows together, adding the corners last (fig. 5).

Note: The triangles are large so that background fabric surrounds the Calico Cat along the edges.

Finishing the Quilt

Layer with batting and backing and quilt.

Cut (6) 2½" x 40" strips to use for the binding. Join end-to-end and add to the quilt.

ABOUT THE AUTHOR

Anne was born in North Carolina, but has lived and worked in the Phoenix area for many years. She began sewing garments at the age of seven without patterns. Her mother taught her that the inside had to look as good as the outside. She took a home economics class in high school where she had to learn to use a pattern. This gave her the idea to focus on order and efficiency in sewing. This translated into the patterns she developed to enhance her quilting endeavors.

She continues to sew clothes for herself and her family and does many forms of needlework as well as quilting, which she started in 1980. She has been influenced by her mother, her grandmother, the late Laureen Senima at the Quilted Apple, and the late Mary Ellen Hopkins.

In 1982, while still working as a critical care nurse, several friends asked if she would like to open a quilt store with them. They pooled their resources, researched how to run a shop, and the *Quilters' Ranch* opened. Anne retired from nursing and to help run the shop for fifteen years. It is still a viable store in the Phoenix area with new owners. In 1994, Anne developed Triangles on a Roll, a paper piecing method of making half-square triangles. She wrote several books and patterns on how to use the product.

She has since sold this business, but this product remains on the market.

Anne's viewpoint on quilts is that they belong on the bed, wrapping loved ones in the comfort and love a quilt provides. She has also designed many quilted garments, wallhangings, art, and memory quilts which offer great variety to the quiltmaker. Over the years of teaching quilting, Anne made three important discoveries. She discovered that quilt making is where friendships are made and the customer is boss. Anne also discovered that the rewards of teaching occur when students realize their dreams and passions and are proud of their quilts.

Anne lives north of Phoenix in the desert foothills with her husband, Virgil, who is her greatest supporter of all things quilting. She continues to teach quilting classes, develop patterns, and welcomes sewing groups to her spacious home for sew-ins and retreats.

PHOTO: Karen Newberg, Secure Observations

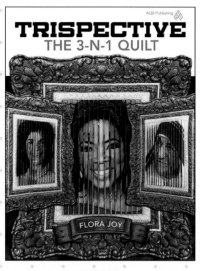

#10281

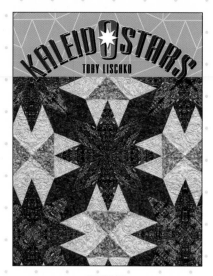

#10283

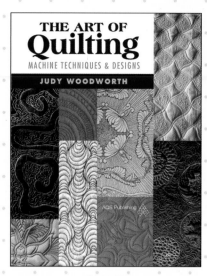

#11140

#10272

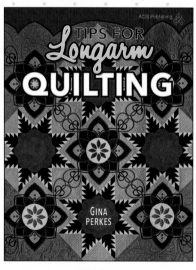

#10285

#10757